Don't Touch Me!

Say No To Sexual Harassment

Orvie B. Baker, Jr.

THE EINMALIG GROUP, LLC

ISBN: 978-0-9857037-3-8

Library of Congress Control Number: 20112913285

PRINTED IN THE UNITED STATES OF AMERICA

My goal is to ensure you know it is your right to live a life free of sexual harassment and sexual assault. My mission is to help provide an environment extremely uncomfortable for sexual predators and predatory behaviors.

-Orvie B. Baker, Jr.

TABLE OF CONTENTS

WHAT IS SEXUAL HARASSMENT?

Army Regulation (AR) 600-20 defines sexual harassment as a form of gender discrimination that involves unwelcome sexual advances, requests for sexual favors, and other verbal or physical conduct of a sexual nature between the same or opposite genders. This book was written to help fight sexual harassment in schools by providing young girls simple rules of engagement.

Practically the norm, Sexual Harassment is becoming commonplace in most middle and high schools. In the Huffington post online report, during the 2010-2011 school year 58 percent of girls and 40 percent of boys said they had experienced at least one incident of sexual harassment during the school year. The American Association of University Women (AAUW) in a recent study found that Harassers are part of a vicious cycle. Most students who admitted to sexually harassing students were the targets of sexual harassment themselves. Sexual Harassment is very similar to Bullying; both are constantly reported in the news and have been blamed in high profile murder and suicide reports.

There are many books and web sites that explain the dangers of sexual harassment; education is essential in combating sexual harassment, but defining it is not enough.

Ten years of teaching Sexual Harassment and Assault Prevention Programs has taught me two things:

- Most offenders target people who present the least resistance
- Many people who have been sexually harassed and/or assaulted

feel they are to blame

The four things I want you, the reader, to take away from this book are:

    I.   There are NO excuses for sexual harassment.
    II.   It is your right to live free of sexual harassment and/or assault.
    III.   The victim of sexual harassment and/or assault is NEVER at fault for what happened to him or her.
    IV.   You have the right to say, "DON'T TOUCH ME!"

The stages to remember when defending against would be harassers:

    a. Verbal Warning
    b. Inform Someone
    c. Self-Defense

VERBAL WARNING

Sexual Harassment has become a part of middle school and high school life over the last several decades. It's portrayed in books, movies, commercials and music videos as flirting. Regardless of a person's intent, if his or her actions are unwanted and sexual in nature, it is considered sexual harassment.

The first step in defending yourself would be giving a verbal warning to the harasser. A verbal warning is a direct approach to inform the harasser you do not like his or her actions and you want it to stop.

Before giving a verbal warning take into consideration your location and who else may hear your verbal warning. A verbal warning not only lets the harasser know you have a problem with their actions, it also let everyone within earshot know you want the behavior to stop.

Clearly state that you don't appreciate being talked to or touched by them. Often, the louder you address the harasser, the more likely it is that they will leave to avoid embarrassment.

Do not be afraid to use your voice as a weapon. This will bring all the attention to the harasser, letting everyone know someone is bothering you and you want the unwanted action to stop, NOW.

INFORM SOMEONE

If the harasser ignores your warning and continues to make unwanted advances, the next step is to gain assistance from another person. Talk with friends who may have seen or heard what happened. Your friends can help you get the message across. Your friends can also alert the proper authorities.

Title IX of the Education Amendments of 1972 require schools to take immediate and effective steps to end sexual harassment and violence. In short, the law is on your side.

Involve the adults who are part of the administration; a teacher, counselor, principal or law enforcement officer has an obligation to step in and help protect you from any form of sexual harassment, but they can only help when they know what is going on.

Last, but not least, involve your parents. Like your school administrators your parents can only get involved and help when they are aware that you are being harassed. Many harassers are opportunistic bullies, and will only bother people who won't get them in trouble or "snitch." The more people know about the unwanted attention, the less likely they (the harassers) will be to harass you.

INFORM SOMEONE

If the harasser ignores your warning and continues to make unwanted advances, the next step is to gain assistance from another person. Talk with friends who may have seen or heard what happened. Your friends can help you get the message across. Your friends can also alert the proper authorities.

Title IX of the Education Amendments of 1972 require schools to take immediate and effective steps to end sexual harassment and violence. In short, the law is on your side.

Involve the adults who are part of the administration; a teacher, counselor, principal or law enforcement officer has an obligation to step in and help protect you from any form of sexual harassment, but they can only help when they know what is going on.

Last, but not least, involve your parents. Like your school administrators your parents can only get involved and help when they are aware that you are being harassed. Many harassers are opportunistic bullies, and will only bother people who won't get them in trouble or "snitch." The more people know about the unwanted attention, the less likely they (the harassers) will be to harass you.

SELF-DEFENSE

So, you have confronted the harasser, told family, friends, and the school administration about the harassment, but you are still being harassed? Now it is time defend yourself! Sometimes you have no other choice but to defend yourself through the use of physical force.

Avoidance is not always possible and if you are continually harassed you have the right to defend yourself. Don't wait until you are in an unavoidable situation; decide what you will do to defend yourself now.

Effective self-defense is achieved through training, which will build confidence and give you a feeling of empowerment.

Martial arts and self-defense courses effectively help you learn to defend yourself and will prevent you from injuring yourself.

Although you can learn a lot from books, TV and the internet, the best way to learn effective self-defense techniques is to sign up for classes at a nearby gym, dojo or recreation center. Many self-defense courses will teach you to use your hands, feet, and available resources to defend yourself, but you may already have defensive techniques of your own; if so, use them! Screaming at an attacker is used as a defensive move; swinging a purse or school bag, wielding an umbrella, using a loud pitch whistle, lodging keys between your knuckles, and/or pepper spray can effectively let the offender know you will not allow anyone to disrespect or inappropriately touch you.

TYPE OF STRIKES:

Palm Heel Strike—With fingers curled under, thumb pressed beside curled index finger, and palm of hand facing downward, rotate wrist upward exposing bottom of hand. This bottom portion of the hand or 'palm heel' is use to strike targets with minimum damage to hand and wrist.

Hammer Fist Strike—Curl fingers inward tightly, so hand is fashioned as a fist. The 'hammer fist' utilizes the bottom and or top of the fist to avoid damage to the knuckles or wrist.

Ridge Hand Strike—With palms facing downward, fingers extended and tightly joined, the 'ridge hand' is utilized by striking a target area with the inside portion of the hand along the palm to little finger. Also known as a karate chop. An effective variation of the ridge hand strike is to face the palms downward, tuck thumb under fingers and use ridge formed along the index finger to strike a target.

Spear Finger Strike—Similar to the ridge hand strike, except the tips of the fingers are used to strike a target area. Variations of the spear finger strike are utilizing only the middle and index fingers spread apart or tightly joined.

Elbow Strike—Utilizing the pointed portion of the elbow to strike close target areas.

Knee Strike—Utilizing the top portion of the knee to strike close target areas.

TARGET AREAS:

Eyes—Use Spear Finger Strikes, Palm Heel Strikes, Elbow and Knee Strikes.

Ears—Use Hammer Fist Strikes, Elbow and Knee Strikes, or cup hands and slap one ear or both ears simultaneously.

Bridge of Nose—Use Palm Heel Strikes, Elbow and Knee Strikes or Hammer Fist Strikes.

Chin—Use Palm Heel Strikes, Hammer Fist Strikes, or Elbow or Knee Strikes.

Windpipe—Use Ridge Hand Strikes, Spear Finger Strikes, Elbow or Knee Strikes.

Groin—Use Knee Strikes, Hammer Fist Strikes or kick with foot.

Knee—Use foot to kick inside or outside area of knee.

Shin—Use foot to kick front area of shinbone or stomp down, scraping the front of shin with shoes.

Top of Foot or Instep—Use foot to stomp down on Instep; heels are very effective when used to stomp on top of foot or instep.

Practice, Learn, Teach... Knowing what sexual harassment is and how to combat it is only the first step. Practicing what you learn will make your reactions more proficient. Always seek out knowledge; learning more about defense against sexual harassment will leave you better equipped to handle it successfully. Teach what you know; not only to help others defend themselves, but to prevent others from committing acts of sexual harassment. Together we can help denounce sexual harassment.

Be an **A.C.E.!**

Aware of the situation and your surroundings

Combat all forms of sexual harassment

Educate others to join the fight and eliminate sexual harassment

"Don't Touch Me!" Let's make it our mission to ensure everyone knows that we stand against sexual harassment.

RESOURCES TO HELP EDUCATE
AND COMBAT SEXUAL VIOLENCE:

Catharsis Productions
http://www.catharsisproductions.com

National Organization for Victim Assistance
http://www.trynova.org

Rape Abuse and Incest National Network
https://www.rainn.org/

Office for Victims of Crime
https://www.ovc.gov/

Battered Women's Justice Project
http://www.bwjp.org/

Safe Help Line
https://www.safehelpline.org/

Department of Defense Sexual Assault Prevention and Response Office
http://www.sapr.mil/

www.ingramcontent.com/pod-product-compliance
Lightning Source LLC
LaVergne TN
LVHW072124070426
835511LV00002B/81